The Young Adventurer's Guide to

REST

FROM AVALANCHE TO ZOPKIO

Jonathan Chester

GREYSTONE BOOKS
Douglas & McIntyre
PUBLISHING GROUP
VANCOUVER / TORONTO

I looked up and there above us was a rounded snow cone . . .
A few whacks of the ice axe, a few cautious steps
and Tenzing and I were on top.

— Sir Edmund Hillary, *High Adventure*

Young adventurers,

One day you may be like Sir Edmund Hillary and stand on top of Mount Everest. But what is it like? How do you get started? What do you need to know?

Read this book, and you will find out. Included here are nuggets of information about the Everest experience, gear lists and resources for tackling the climb, and of course plenty of pictures to whet your appetite.

When I was a boy, I loved the outdoors. I used to roam the hills and valleys outside my hometown of Adelaide, South Australia, in search of adventure. I loved the excitement of exploring new places, especially camping and hiking, and sleeping in tents or under the stars.

When I grew older, I became hooked on climbing. I set off on a lifelong quest for adventure that has taken me on expeditions to all seven continents.

You too can have a life of adventure and exploration. Pick up your ice axe. Strap on your crampons. Let's begin!

Jonathan Chester

LEFT: Me on the summit of Broad Peak at 26,402 feet (8,047 meters) in Pakistan.

Avalanches

Watch out for avalanches. They are extremely dangerous. One of the most awesome spectacles in the Himalayas, an avalanche is a mass of snow, rock, and ice that cascades down a mountainside. A small ice fragment or a rock hitting a slope high up on the mountain may trigger a snow slide that can rapidly gain momentum until it overwhelms everything in its path.

What do you do if you're caught in an avalanche?

Try swimming on its surface by doing the breaststroke and kicking to keep your head above the snow. If you are buried in an avalanche, try to guard your face and create an air pocket by pushing the snow away from your mouth.

The roar was tremendous...
like the sound of bombs bursting
in a hundred thunderstorms.

— Ed Bernbaum,
Sacred Mountains of the World

Base Camp

If you make it this far, you are doing well. At an elevation of 17,600 feet (5,364 meters) on the very rocky edge of the Khumbu Glacier, Everest Base Camp is the first major goal for climbers. It serves as a resting place and a supply depot. Many climbers from around the world camp here during the spring and fall climbing seasons, creating a temporary village of 300 to 600 people. Base Camp is as big as several football fields, with tents and shelters of all shapes and sizes perched on rocky platforms.

5,364 meters

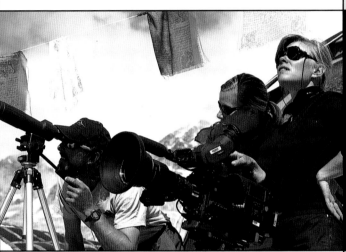

17,600 feet

When the climbing team is in Base Camp, meals are the main focus of the day. Breakfast is usually cereal and fried eggs. Lunch and dinner are often Spam, potatoes, and Tibetan bread.

At Base Camp you join mountaineers, scientists, photographers, and journalists in the special communications tent that houses the VHF radio base station and sometimes a satellite telephone.

You share computers for digital photography, research, and to send e-mail to family and friends. Sometimes at night, when it is too cold to work, you can even watch a DVD movie.

Crevasses

If you think avalanches are dangerous, try crevasses. A crevasse is a split or crack in the ice that occurs when a glacier moves or twists around a bend or over a giant rock formation. A crevasse can be narrow enough to jump across or as wide as a small valley. A thin covering of snow sometimes conceals crevasses, which is why they are so treacherous.

To travel safely through crevassed terrain, you need to be roped to one or two partners, and the leader needs to probe the surface of the snow with an ice axe or ski pole if the terrain looks suspicious. If you fall into a crevasse that is 100 feet (30 meters) deep without being roped to your partner, who could stop the fall or pull you out, it is unlikely that you would survive.

BELOW: Blind mountaineer Erik Weihenmayer crosses one of the many ladders used to bridge the wider crevasses in the Khumbu Icefall. Fellow climber Eric Alexander follows.

Down suits

You can never wear enough clothing on Everest. High up on the mountain, the biting winds and extreme cold can suck the heat out of you very rapidly. Tiny goose feathers called down, which trap lots of air when they are fluffed up, are the best insulation. A one-piece Gore-Tex oversuit lined with plenty of high-quality down is the warmest, lightest garment you can use. It's like wearing a very warm sleeping bag. On down suits, zippers and Velcro are strategically located to enable you to go to the toilet without having to get fully undressed. You should wear a bright-colored down suit so that you can be seen more easily in bad weather and poor light in case you get lost or are stranded and need to be rescued.

ABOVE: While photographing the climbers at the foot of the icefall, it was cold enough for me to wear my trusty down suit.

What is so special about Mount Everest?

For starters, it is the highest mountain in the world and one of the most challenging to climb. Why is Mount Everest so dangerous? Well, you can take a deadly fall, because in many places it is very steep; you can be buried in an avalanche; you can plummet into a crevasse; or you can be stranded in a freezing storm with lightning, thunder, and high winds. Mount Everest tests your physical limits, because at the summit the temperature is well below freezing and the oxygen level is one-third that of sea level. The low oxygen level and cold make it very difficult to catch your breath, and you can only move at a snail's pace.

Early expeditions to Mount Everest approached the mountain from the north side through Tibet. The most legendary of these was the ill-fated attempt in 1924 by George Mallory and Andrew Irving. Both disappeared, and Mallory's body wasn't discovered until 1999. It has never been determined whether he was on the way up or down from the summit. Mallory is famous for saying, when asked why he wanted to climb Mount Everest, "Because it is there."

The two main climbing seasons on Mount Everest are spring and fall, or premonsoon and postmonsoon. Before starting to climb Mount Everest you need to get a permit from either the Nepalese or the Chinese government, depending which side you will climb. Both countries require that a government representative accompany the expedition.

EVEREST FACTS

Height: 29,035 feet (8,850 meters)
5.5 miles (8.85 kilometers) above sea level

Location: Latitude 27°59'16" North
Longitude 86°55'40" East
On the border between Nepal and China

Movements: Growing about 1/6 inch
(4 millimeters) per year
Moving northeast at 2-1/3 inches
(6 centimeters) per year

Names: Mount Everest, once known as Peak 15, is named after Sir George Everest (1790-1866, the British Surveyor General of India, in charge of mapping the subcontinent)
Sagamartha (Nepali)
means "Forehead in the Sky"
Chomolungma (Tibetan)
means "Goddess Mother of the World"

GETTING TO THE TOP

First: May 29, 1953 via Western Cwm and South Col by Sir Edmund Hillary (New Zealand) and Tenzing Norgay (Nepal)

First woman: May 16, 1975 by Junko Tabei (Japan)

First without supplementary oxygen: August 5, 1978 by Reinhold Messner (Italy) and Peter Habler (Austria)

First solo: August 8, 1980 by Reinhold Messner (Italy)

Most: 11 by Apa Sherpa (Nepal)

Fastest: May 20, 2000 by Babu Chiri Sherpa (Nepal), 16 hours, 56 minutes—from Base Camp

Youngest: May 22, 2001 by Temba Tsheri Sherpa (Nepal), age 15

Oldest: May 25, 2001 by Sherman Bull (United States), age 64

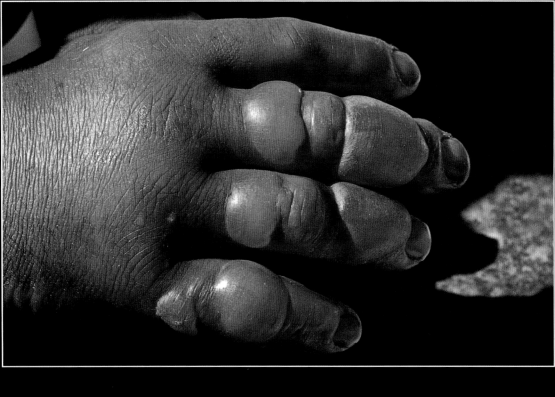

Frostbite

Getting very cold can be deadly. Frostbite occurs when your extremities become so cold that they freeze. It most often happens to hands, feet, nose, and ears if they are not properly protected in very cold, windy conditions. First you lose feeling in the affected part, and then it becomes white and waxy looking. If you get frostbite, do not attempt to rewarm the affected parts until you are out of danger and preferably with caregivers. It is better to walk on frozen feet than to risk them refreezing if you have thawed them out. Rewarming is very painful and is usually accompanied by a lot of swelling. Typically rewarming is carried out in a bath of warm water.

After you rewarm your frostbitten extremities, water-filled blisters appear, and there is the danger of infection. Very serious frostbite cases can result in losing parts of your fingers and toes. When this happens, first the frostbitten tissue dries out, and it turns black. Eventually the dead flesh falls off after a few weeks or months.

ABOVE: This is actually my hand. As bad as it looks, I ended up losing only the very tip of one finger, and I am

Gear

On Mount Everest you need the lightest, warmest, most durable gear possible. You have to be self-sufficient for at least two months, as there are no stores from which to resupply.

This well dressed Everest climber, Charley Mace, wears a one-piece Gore-Tex wind-suit, a harness around the waist at all times, a Jumar for attaching to the rope in the Icefall and on steep slopes. The white silk scarf (kata) is a gift from the Sherpas for good luck.

what do you take

1 NANCY FEAGIN IN FULL GEAR
Dressed for the Khumbu Icefall, top U.S. climber, Nancy Feagin, is on her way to the summit. Climbing harness, carabiners, Jumar, descender, treking pole, and slings are all standard wear when mountaineering.

2 COMMUNICATIONS DOME WITH SOLAR PANELS
A large dome tent for working and socializing is great for morale and getting things done in bad weather. Solar panels used with a car battery give an environmentally friendly source of power to run radios, lights, and computers.

3 GAMOW BAG
Named after its inventor Igor Gamow, this lightweight collapsible pressuriza-tion chamber is used to treat altitude sickness.

4 DOUBLE BOOTS
High altitude mountaineering boots have three layers: an inner boot made of foam, an outer boot made of plastic or leather, and an insulated Gore-Tex overgaiter that is sometimes part of the boot.

5 ICE AXE AND MITTEN
Your ice axe is your main means of assistance when mountaineering. It can be a walking stick, useful for swinging into steep ice to pull yourself up on, or finally as a belay (anchor). Insulated mittens are worn over one or two layers of synthetic inner gloves.

6 BOWLINE
Climbing ropes are between 9.8 and 11 millimeters in diameter and are very strong. The two main knots used in climbing are the bowline and the figure-of-eight.

7 ALTIMETER / WATCH
Being able to track your altitude can be of great assistance on the climb. These watches can also work as a barometer helping you monitor the weather.

8 SLEEPING BAG
Very warm mountain sleeping bags made of high grade down weigh about 4 pounds (2 kilograms).

9 GPS AND MAP
Using a map and Global Positioning System (GPS) unit to learn the lay of the mountain will be of great help if you get caught in a storm.

for such a climb?

6

7

8

9

EVEREST EQUIPMENT

BASIC KIT
Duffel bags (3)
Daypack
Climbing pack
Summit pack

SLEEPING GEAR
Sleeping bag (trek)
Sleeping bag (mountain)
Thick foam pad
Self-inflating pad
Inner sheet
Pillow

SHELTER
Base Camp tent
Gore-Tex bivy bag

FOOTWEAR
Running shoes
Hiking boots
Flip-flops
Double boots
Insulated booties
Snow gaiters

EYE PROTECTION
Clear goggles
Tinted goggles
Sunglasses
Glacier glasses

CLOTHING
Sun hat
Baseball cap
Bandanna
Balaclava
Ski hat

Glove liners
Expedition gloves
Fleece mittens
Cotton socks (3 pairs)
Hiking socks (3 pairs)
Sock liners (3 pairs)
Underwear (4 sets)
Long-sleeved shirt
T-shirts (2)
Hiking shorts (2)
Lightweight pants
Heavy tops (2)
Heavy bottoms (2)
Long white underwear
Swimsuit

OUTERWEAR
Gore-Tex jacket
Light Gore-Tex pants
Gore-Tex parka
Gore-Tex bibs
Gore-Tex wind suit
Fleece jacket
Fleece vest
Fleece pants
Down suit
Down jacket

MISCELLANEOUS
Toiletries
Towel
Sewing and repair kit
First aid kit
Insect repellent
Toilet paper
Flashlight

Batteries
Water bottles (3)
Hydration system
Pee bottle
Insulated mug
Eating utensils
Plastic bags
Altimeter watch
Alarm clock
Binoculars
Books
Candle and matches
CD player and discs
Nylon cord
Compass
GPS and maps
Journal and pens
Nylon stuff bags
Swiss army knife
Umbrella
Cameras
Film

CLIMBING GEAR
Ice axe
Ice hammer
Trekking poles
Crampons (2 pairs)
Waist harness
Figure 8 descender
Belay device
Locking carabiners (2)
Carabiners (10)
Ice screws
Crampon protectors

Head lamp
Helmet
Jumar ascenders
Rescue pulley

TEAM EQUIPMENT
Mountain tents
Mountain pots
Gas stoves
Climbing ropes
Fixed ropes
Deadmen
Ice screws
Pitons
Marker wands
Snow shovels
Snow stakes
Radios (handheld)
Radio base station
Satellite telephone
Solar panels
Car battery
Communications dome
Cooking/eating tents
Base Camp cook pots
Stoves
Gamow bag
Group First Aid Kit
Pressure lanterns
Repair kits
Tables and stools
Storage tents
Tarps

Pilots don't fly through clouds in the Himalayas because the clouds have rocks in them. — Anonymous

Helicopters

What happens if you get sick or hurt?

High on Mount Everest there is little hope of rescue. Lower down you stand a chance of being helped.

Helicopters are often used in the Everest region of Nepal to evacuate injured or ill climbers and trekkers and occasionally for sightseeing. Helicopters fly up and down the valley early in the morning, when the sky is usually clearer and the air more dense. Khumbu Base Camp, at 17,600 feet (5,364 meters), is at the upper limit of regular helicopter operations. Any higher the air is too thin for the necessary lift.

Charter helicopter flights also carry expedition equipment to and from Sangboche—the small landing strip just above Namche Bazaar, the main center in the Khumbu region—saving many days of load carrying by porters or yaks. Occasionally, you can also get a ride on one of these spectacular cargo flights.

SPOT THE CLIMBERS!

Ice

Imagine being surrounded on all sides by ice, ice, and more ice. It's like moving through a giant freezer that badly needs defrosting. Most of Mount Everest is covered with ice that never melts. The main route from the south (Nepal) side involves climbing the **Khumbu Icefall.** This is where the glacier flowing out of the Western Cwm (pronounced "koom" which is Welsh for a valley ringed with mountains) tumbles steeply 2,000 feet (600 meters) in a jumble of crevasses and seracs (ice towers). The glacier travels about 3 feet (1 meter) per day, which means that the route is constantly changing. The Khumbu Icefall is a frightening place to be because it creaks and groans, indicating just how much it is moving. You need to be able to climb quickly in order to minimize the time you are at risk from the falling ice towers and gaping crevasses. Only one route, which everyone shares, is maintained through the icefall. You use fixed ropes as handrails to get up the ice faces, and you cross many aluminum ladders over vast chasms. These aids are installed at the beginning of each climbing season by a team of Sherpas led by Ang Nima, also known as the "icefall doctor." He has been maintaining this route for twenty-five years.

Juniper

Is Mount Everest a sacred mountain?

As you trek to Everest and hike above the pine forests, you see hillsides covered in low, shrubby trees called juniper. These trees have a role in Tibetan Buddhist religious ceremonies.

For many people, especially the Sherpas, climbing Mount Everest is a spiritual experience, but Everest itself is not a sacred mountain. Soon after teams arrive at Base Camp, a special ceremony called a puja is held at the small stone altar, or chorten, built in each camp.

The chorten is easily located because of the long strings of prayer flags radiating from it. Here a Lama (Tibetan Buddhist priest) asks the gods for understanding and toleration of the climb. All the team and their equipment are blessed. The gear is passed through the smoke of the burning juniper branches, bathing it in a protective coat of incense. The Sherpas believe that the thick smoke clears the way for favorable events.

As the expedition progresses and climbers head up the mountain from Base Camp, the Sherpas observe their spiritual duties with a small ceremony, burning more juniper and making an offering to seek blessings from the gods.

> *K2 stood over us, remote and chill, yet more beautiful than any other mountain.*
> *A symbol it seemed, of all that is unattainable. An eternal temptation.*
>
> — Kurt Diemberger, *The Endless Knot*

K2

After you have climbed Mount Everest, what is left to do?

Many mountaineers who climb Everest try for the "seven summits," the highest peaks on all seven continents. The most serious climbers often go on to the greater challenge of K2, nicknamed the Savage Mountain.

K2, at 28,267 feet (8,616 meters) in the Karakoram Range, is the world's second highest mountain. However, even by its easiest route, the Abruzzi Ridge, K2 is widely accepted as a much more difficult climb than Mount Everest. This is why K2 is called the mountain of mountains. It was first climbed in 1954 by a large Italian expedition led by Ardito Desio.

K2 has had only about 200 ascents and yet has claimed fifty lives. Its steepness, extreme altitude, and wild weather have contributed to the low success rate and high death rate of expeditions. K2 is a real climber's mountain and not a place for amateurs on guided teams.

K2 straddles the border between China and Pakistan, and the approach from either side is long and potentially dangerous. On the southern (Pakistan) side, the trek is up the mighty Baltoro Glacier. From China the approach is via the Shaksgam Valley, and camels are used rather than porters.

Lukla

Getting to the mountains from Kathmandu, the main entry point and capital of Nepal, is not easy. In the past it was a day's bus ride on narrow, bumpy dirt roads just to get to the start of the trek. Today you fly to Lukla (9,350 feet, or 2,850 meters), a bustling village with dozens of lodges and hotels. It is now the main gateway to Mount Everest and the Khumbu region for trekkers and climbers. Traditionally the trek began at Jiri, a week's walk to the south of Lukla. Sir Edmund Hillary and friends built the short Lukla airstrip in 1964 to assist in the delivery of building supplies to the region. Today the steeply angled airstrip is paved and handles up to a dozen helicopter or small plane flights a day at its busiest. A landing here is one of the most exciting you will ever have on a commercial airplane. The runway is perched on a steeply rising ridgetop and ends at a cliff face that your plane could smack into if your pilot overshoots the landing. There are no second chances with this airstrip, and the weather is often cloudy or raining.

From Lukla it is about a ten- to fourteen-day walk to Everest Base Camp. Typically a porter or yak carries most of your load. If you are part of a self-contained trek or expedition group, you will probably camp, but many individuals and groups choose to stay in the numerous lodges in the villages along the trail.

Landing at Lukla is like parking your car in a garage at 80 mph.

— Anonymous

Mani stones

On the way to Everest, you encounter many mysterious things. Some of the more unusual are the intricately carved Mani stones. These are rocks inscribed with special Tibetan Buddhist prayers, or sacred spells called mantras. The most common mantra is "Om Mani Padme Hum" (Hail to the Jewel in Lotus). It is also very common to hear the Sherpas chanting this prayer.

The symbols and words are found carved into everything from small flat stones to giant boulders and rock faces in the Buddhist areas of the Himalayas. Individual stones are often arranged in low walls with paths on both sides. Although Hindu porters do not observe Tibetan Buddhist tradition, out of respect, you should always pass the Mani wall clockwise with the wall on your right side.

Namche Bazaar

After two days of trekking above Lukla, just when you think you are getting away from civilization, you arrive at Namche. Namche Bazaar (11,319 feet, or 3,450 meters) is the capital of the Khumbu region. With its numerous shops and lodges and a bustling Saturday market, it's an exciting spot for climbers and trekkers to spend several days getting used to the altitude. After the steep hike up from the Dudh Kosi (river), when you first arrive you may be exhausted or even have a splitting headache. Once you adjust to the thin air, you will want to explore Tibetan culture by visiting a Gompa, or museum, shopping for souvenirs or buying last minute items of climbing and trekking gear. The colorful street stalls in the narrow alleys are bulging with everything from Thankas (religious paintings) and T-shirts to maps and mittens.

You can also spend time at one of the many bakeries that have sprung up. You can send and receive e-mail at a cybercafé in a small room at the back of a Western-style bar. However, the Internet connection is via an ancient satellite dish, so it is slow and expensive. Sooner or later it's time to hit the trail again and leave this oasis of civilization behind.

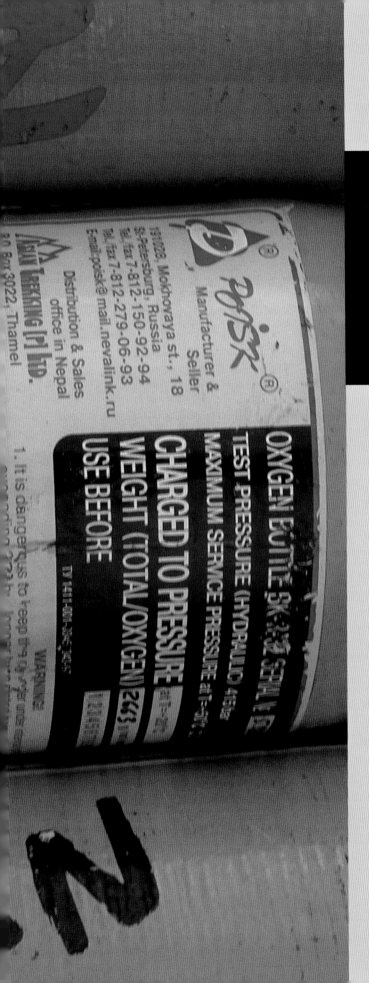

Climbing above 26,000 feet even with bottled oxygen is like running on a treadmill and breathing through a straw.

— David Breashears, in *Everest: Mountain Without Mercy*

Oxygen

Why is it so hard to breathe on the summit?

The reduced air pressure at the top of Mount Everest means that there is only one-third the amount of oxygen that there is at sea level. Above 26,240 feet (8,000 meters) is often referred to as the **Death Zone.** You have to spend as little time as possible in the Death Zone, going up and down quickly, otherwise you will get weaker and weaker and eventually die. To increase their chance of success, most climbers use bottled oxygen when going for the top.

Today's oxygen systems for climbing are lightweight. When full, a bottle, valve, and mask weighs around 8 pounds (3.6 kilograms). The pure oxygen mixes with regular air in the face mask system when you inhale. While sleeping at Camp III and Camp IV, you will use a flow rate of 1 liter per minute, but when climbing you need to increase the flow to 2 to 4 liters per minute. A bottle will last you approximately three to six hours. Most climbers consume at least three bottles going from the South Col to the top and back down again. On the way up, one of these is often left by the trail for the return journey.

Porters

It is hard to believe that so much gear and equipment gets moved to Mount Everest and back again when there are no roads. Yet every day professional load carriers, called porters, carry everything you can imagine in this part of the world, from firewood to building materials, expedition gear, and even other people.

The porters of Nepal are some of the hardiest people you will ever meet. They can be from any number of different ethnic groups such as the Rais, Limbu, or Sherpas, but typically Sherpas work as high-altitude porters on expeditions. Porters carry their enormous loads with long straps called tumplines bearing all the weight on their foreheads. Sometimes they also use a cone-shaped basket woven out of bamboo called a doko. A normal porter load is 45 pounds (20 kilograms), for which the porter is paid about $4.50 per day. This is good pay by local standards. If porters are going to carry your loads all the way to Base Camp, you need to make sure that they are properly equipped in case there is a storm.

Quomolangma

Quomolangma is the Chinese spelling of Chomolungma (Goddess Mother of the Earth), the Tibetan and Sherpa name for Mount Everest.

From the west and north of the Tibetan side, particularly the valley of Rongbuk, Quomolangma can be seen from a great distance as an imposing pyramid of rock and ice. Two sides of the pyramid, the Kangshung and the Northwest Face, are in Tibet.

The very first attempts to climb Quomolangma were from Tibet, and there are seven routes on the north and east sides. The Chinese were the first to climb to the summit from the north side via the North and Northeast Ridges in 1960.

It is possible to drive to several of the base camps on the Tibetan side, but the roads often wash out in the postmonsoon season. Today the Chinese Mountaineering Association oversees all the climbing from the north, and once all of the costs are included, it is as expensive to climb from the Tibetan side as from Nepal.

BELOW: North and west sides of Quomolangma

Route

This description is by filmmaker Michael Brown, who climbed to the summit of Mount Everest in the spring season's of 2000 and 2001.

In your climb of Everest you will spend several months acclimatizing and establishing camps with the help of your Sherpas. In the course of this work you will pass up and down the route, working your way higher and higher until at last you are ready for the summit push.

From Base Camp to Camp I (19,000 feet, or 5,945 meters): The main route up Mount Everest from the southern (Nepal) side begins at Everest Base Camp (17,600 feet, or 5,364 meters). The path winds through the treacherous Khumbu Icefall before reaching Camp I at 19,500 feet (5,943 meters). When you are first on the mountain it takes the better part of a day to get to Camp I.

From Camp I to II (21,300 feet, or 6,942 meters): The route ascends into the Western Cwm, a sloping U-shaped valley. Once you are better acclimatized, on subsequent ascents, you will probably skip Camp I and go directly to Camp II in one push.

Camp II to Camp III (24,000 feet, or 7,315 meters): The Cwm continues for a thousand vertical feet in about a half mile above Camp II; then the route changes abruptly to a steep ice ramp, the Lhotse Face. It is over a vertical mile high to the top of the world's fourth highest peak, Lhotse. Camp III sits halfway up the Lhotse Face. You have to cut tent spaces out of a 45-degree ice slope.

Camp III to Camp IV (26,000 feet, or 7,925 meters): This is the second hardest day of the climb, with a 2,000-foot gain ending at 26,000 feet of elevation at the South Col. Traversing the Lhotse Face, you cross two rock features that require some technical scrambling. The first is the Yellow Band, a layer of crumbly sedimentary rock at 24,500 feet (7,500 meters). The second is the Geneva Spur.

From the top of the Geneva Spur, the route follows exposed rock shelves for about a half mile before arriving in the South Col and Camp IV.

Camp IV to Summit (29,035 feet, or 8,850 meters, and back): Early in the evening, around 8:30 P.M., you will start getting ready, filling water bottles, harnessing up, and putting on crampons. By 10:00 P.M. you will hopefully be moving upward. The climb starts out easily enough, and it is refreshingly cool.

Above the Col there is an ice bulge of hard blue ice followed by a long, gradual snow slope. Across a bergshrund there is a steep gully. You hope for snow here, as loose rock or hard ice will be difficult to climb. This section goes on for a very long time with about 1,200 feet (365 meters) of gain. Eventually the slope changes slightly before a last steep pitch to the Balcony at 27,500 feet (8,400 meters). After climbing continuously all night, here you will watch a most spectacular sunrise. By now your pack, oxygen bottle, and down suit is covered in a thick layer of frost.

The climbing above the Balcony starts out easily enough but gets steeper and steeper. Soon you are crossing crumbly rock bands with little snow clinging to them. It is also deceptive, as it seems that you are about to reach the South Summit only to discover that there is another ridge beyond.

The South Summit is at 28,710 feet (8,751 meters), and from there one can see the knife-edge ridge that leads to the Hillary Step and the Summit Ridge. It is a short down climb to this ridge and then a wild walk along the highest exposure on the planet. To the left and 8,000 feet (2,438 meters) down, straight down, is Camp II. To the right is the 12,000-foot (3,660-meter) drop into Tibet.

The Hillary Step is one desperate and very ungraceful move. You stick the crampon point of your left foot tenuously in a tiny crack and your right foot behind you in a cornice of snow. Slide the ascender as high as it will go and then stand up and quickly plant your ice axe before you start sliding down again.

At last you are on the Summit Ridge, a half hour to an hour of slogging uphill to a small mound of snow. Beyond that the ridge drops away into Tibet. This is the top of the world: the summit of Mount Everest. Hopefully, for your sake, you will have lots of oxygen and most of the day left to get back down to Camp IV.

Map labels: N Nepal · CHINA · 30° · HIMALAYA · Karnali · Dhaulagiri+ · Yarlung · NEPAL · Kali Gandak · Mount Everest · Kathmandu · Lukla · Sun Kosi · Gandak · INDIA · ©1999 maps.com · Ganges · 85° · 0 50 100 mi · 0 50 100 km

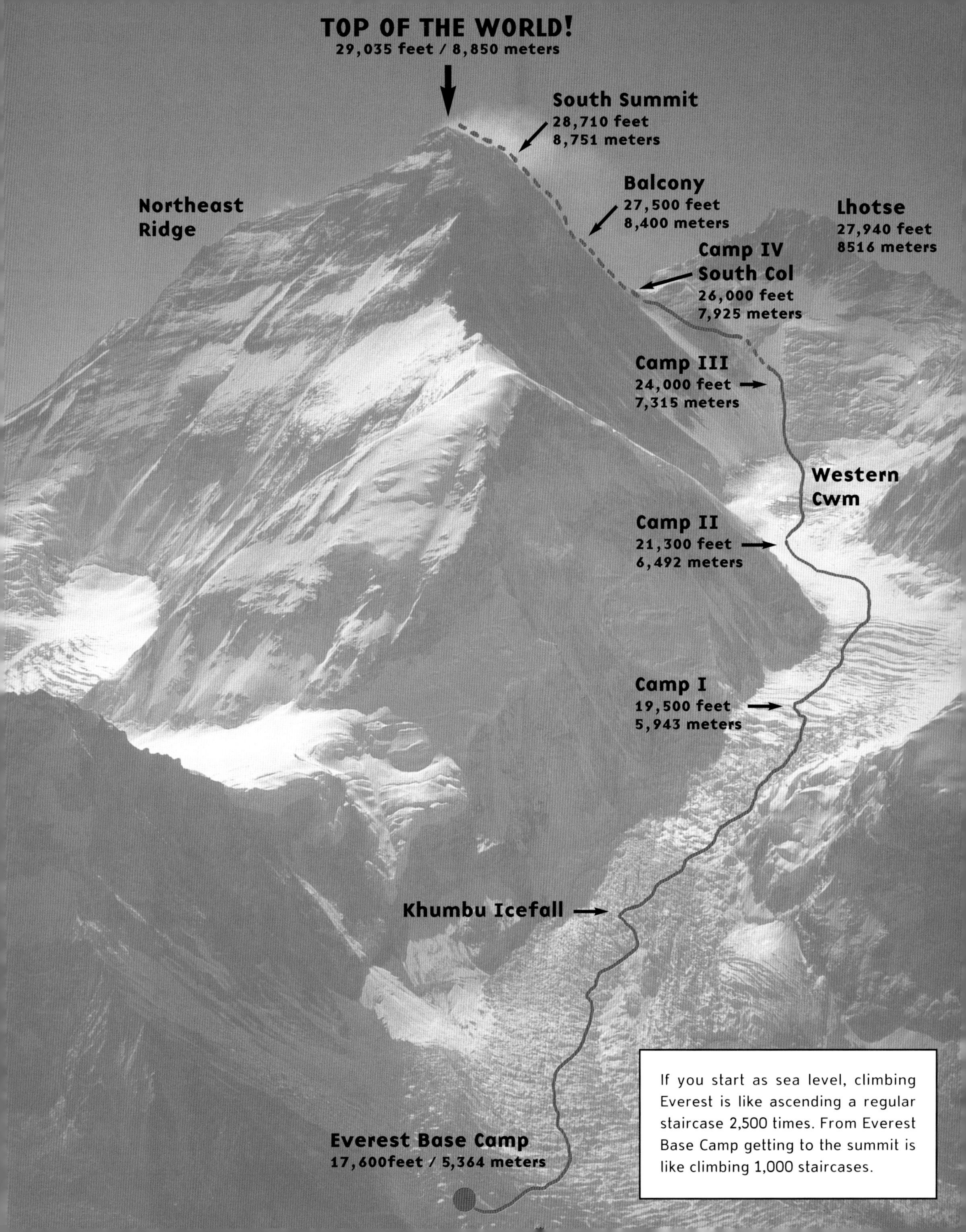

TOP OF THE WORLD!
29,035 feet / 8,850 meters

South Summit
28,710 feet
8,751 meters

Northeast Ridge

Balcony
27,500 feet
8,400 meters

Lhotse
27,940 feet
8516 meters

Camp IV South Col
26,000 feet
7,925 meters

Camp III
24,000 feet
7,315 meters

Western Cwm

Camp II
21,300 feet
6,492 meters

Camp I
19,500 feet
5,943 meters

Khumbu Icefall →

Everest Base Camp
17,600feet / 5,364 meters

If you start as sea level, climbing Everest is like ascending a regular staircase 2,500 times. From Everest Base Camp getting to the summit is like climbing 1,000 staircases.

Sherpas

> *People who climb Everest boast of their success but few of them mention that 95 percent of the work — the grunt work — was done by the Sherpas.*
>
> — Ed Viesturs in *Everest: Mountain Without Mercy*

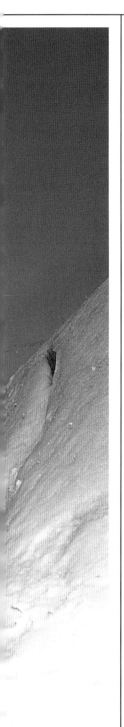

Sherpas typically greet you with gleaming eyes, the warmest smiles, and the strongest handshakes in the world. They are very friendly people. Sherpas come from the mountainous Khumbu area of Nepal. Because they live so high up most of the time at high altitudes, they are much stronger than most Western climbers. The name Sherpa comes from the Tibetan Shar-pa, which means easterner. Sherpa women are called Sherpanis. Few Sherpanis work as guides, but some carry loads to Base Camp or herd yaks for expeditions. Several Sherpanis have reached the summit.

The head Sherpa on an expedition team is called the sirdar. The name sherpa has also become the term used for the position of guide and high-altitude porter on any Himalayan mountaineering team. Today not all people working as sherpas are necessarily from the Sherpa people.

The Sherpa people migrated south from the Tibetan Plateau, where they lived as nomadic herders and traders, roughly 600 years ago. They practice a special form of Buddhism and speak Tibetan. The decline of their salt trade between Tibet and Nepal when the Tibetan border was closed in 1959 was accompanied by a growth in mountaineering and trekking. Sherpa people working as guides have earned a great reputation as tough, cheerful, and honest partners on expeditions. When not trekking or climbing, they work as farmers and yak herders. About 3,000 Sherpas live in the Khumbu, and a total of 35,000 live in Nepal. Many climbers form such strong bonds with the Sherpas who climb Everest with them that those Sherpa friends are invited to join the climbers on expeditions all over the Himalayas.

BOTTOM: Leading sirdar (organizer), Apa Sherpa holds the record for the most summits. He's been to the top eleven times!

The World's Highest Junkyard

*— Barry Bishop describing Camp IV, South Col in 1963
in Everest: Mountain Without Mercy*

Trash

What happens to all the discarded gas stove canisters, oxygen cylinders, sardine cans, toilet paper, and broken tents? For some time now Mount Everest has been called the highest junkyard in the world though expeditions today are much more environmentally responsible and closely monitored than expeditions even ten years ago. Climbing teams have to carry out what they carry into the mountain or risk paying a penalty to the Sagamartha National Park. Consequently trash is now less of a problem than it used to be at Base Camp and Camp II.

There have been numerous so-called cleanup or environmental, expeditions that have had the goal of removing trash, particularly empty oxygen cylinders, from the mountain. Today when Sherpas descend the mountain with light or no loads, they collect and carry down rubbish, which is exchanged for money by a team from the Sagamartha Pollution Control Committee, set up as part of the Sagamartha National Park. This garbage is then removed from Base Camp by yaks or porters. Human waste is collected in garbage bags and is removed in the same way. While the trail to Everest and Base Camp is well looked after, there is still a large amount of trash higher on the mountain. Occasionally, there is even a dead body so frozen into the ice that it cannot be removed. Dead bodies are seldom brought down from higher up.

Underwear

Staying warm on Everest is very difficult. The secret is many layers of very lightweight clothing. The layers trap air (which is the best insulator), yet can also stop the wind. A good set of long underwear made of silk or synthetic material is the best first layer.

At times you can be too hot, such as in the Western Cwm on a windless day when the sun is reflecting off all sides of the icy canyon. Then it is best to strip down to your underwear, which should be white so that some of the heat is reflected off you, but you also need to be completely covered from head to toe to prevent sunburn. The sun's intense rays will fry you if you don't watch out.

Victory!

Why climb Mount Everest?

For some it is for the view, for others the exhilaration, or the sense of victory at overcoming such great odds.

Getting to the very top of Mount Everest is undoubtedly a great triumph, which takes supreme physical effort. The total exhaustion you feel after reaching the summit makes the descent the most dangerous part of the climb. Consequently your time on the summit is usually very brief. On the very top, if the weather is good, you have the most spectacular 360-degree panorama in the world. Most people who make it to the top only feel a real sense of victory when they get back down safely to Base Camp. As Ed Viesturs says, in *Everest: Mountain Without Mercy*, "You don't assault Everest, you sneak up on it, and then get the hell out of there."

Wind

Climbers on Everest are obsessed with weather forecasts, which is hardly surprising as they "live or die" by them.

Everest is extremely windy most of the time. Only in brief periods during the spring and fall does the wind relent a little and these seasons are when most ascents are made. The average wind speed is 50 miles (80 kilometers) per hour. Even the slightest breeze up high sucks heat out of you. This is known as the wind–chill factor, which contributes to the very dangerous lowering of your core body temperature known as hypothermia and to frostbite, which occurs when your fingers and toes begin to freeze.

Mount Everest is so high that it is sometimes also hit by the Jet Stream. This is a large current of very fast moving air traveling from east to west in the upper atmosphere that predominates in winter.

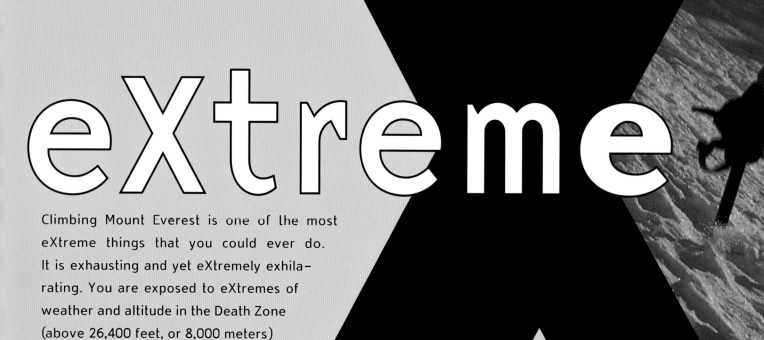

eXtreme

Climbing Mount Everest is one of the most eXtreme things that you could ever do. It is exhausting and yet eXtremely exhilarating. You are exposed to eXtremes of weather and altitude in the Death Zone (above 26,400 feet, or 8,000 meters) for the better part of a day. Everest is eXtremely dangerous—there is about one death for every five successful summits.

Yaks and Zopkios

And you thought yaks were just all talk! Yaks are squat, woolly mammals related to the North American bison that can work at altitudes as high as 20,000 feet (6,096 meters). The Sherpa people use yaks for meat, milk, butter, wool, and ploughing fields, and yaks are the main load carriers in the Khumbu region. Even their dung is burned in cooking fires for heat and warmth. Yaks can carry about 40 to 80 pounds (20 to 40 kilograms) balanced on either side of a wooden saddle. Many yaks come and go on the trail to Everest Base Camp, with one driver per three to five yaks. If a yak is coming toward you, get well out of its way, preferably on the uphill side. Otherwise you risk being knocked off your feet as it brushes past. Yaks do not normally live below about 10,000 feet (3,281 meters) because of their heavy coats, and they are also susceptible to diseases if they move lower down. The Sherpas call females nacks and only the males yaks, but to you and me, they are usually all just yaks.

The ideal load carrier at lower elevations is the zopkio, or zo, a cross between a yak and a cow. Zopkios have lighter coats and are less temperamental than yaks.

How to Get Started

My best advice for a 10-year old who wants to climb? Start practicing in the tree nearest your house. Make sure you're not afraid of heights. If you can, take a class at a local rock climbing gym. — Didrik Johnck, Everest summiteer, 2001

Having learned about Mount Everest from A to Z, you are now raring to go and check out those crampons and ice axes from your nearest climbing store. Before you go rushing off, however, you should learn the ropes from an experienced guide or teacher. There is a lot you still need to know to get started.

There are countless opportunities for you to learn to climb through adventure programs at schools and colleges.

When you are a bit older, a course with Outward Bound or the National Outdoor Leadership School (NOLS) will give you a head start.

You could also join a regional club, many of which have special youth programs. The American Alpine Club (AAC) has no age limit, but prospective members need two years of climbing experience.

Another possibility later on is to learn through a professional mountain-guiding outfitter.

Today, even if you live far from cliffs, there are many gyms with artificial climbing walls that offer classes where you can learn to climb.

Some people get introduced to the Himalayas and Mount Everest through trekking, which requires minimal mountain experience and can be done as a teenager.

Being a strong and safe mountaineer takes years of practice, but there is a lot of fun and adventure to be had along the way.

ABOVE: Professional mountain guide, Mike O'Donnell, front pointing in his double boots with crampons and ice tools on a serac near Everest Base Camp.

Everest Lingo

altitude sickness As you ascend, your body takes time to adjust to the thinner air and reduced level of oxygen. If you go too high too fast, you can get very ill. Common early symptoms are headaches, nausea, and dizziness. Recommended rate of ascent is 1,000 feet (300 meters) per day.

ascender The general name for any mechanical device used to climb up a rope. The first well-known brand was the Jumar, which has become a general term used to describe all such devices.

belay The procedure of securing the lead climber or second (following) climber with a rope.

bergschrund A crevasse that separates two fields of ice in the upper reaches of a glacier.

bivouac (bivy) An unplanned night spent outdoors, usually with minimal equipment.

blizzard A strong windstorm carrying snow or ice particles. A blizzard can reduce visibility to zero (known as a white-out) and make your climb perilous.

carabiner A lightweight aluminum alloy snaplink with a spring-loaded gate.

chorten Tibetan Buddhist stupa or circular stone.

crampons Metal frames with long spikes that can be strapped or clamped to your boots to give you a firm grip when climbing snow and ice.

deadman A spade-shaped lightweight metal plate that is buried in snow to act as a belay anchor.

death zone The region above 26,240 feet (8,000 meters) found on fourteen peaks in the Himalayas where you cannot survive for very long because of the thin air, cold, and extreme weather.

doko A conical cane basket used by porters to carry loads.

edema A pulmonary or cerebral edema is a very serious form of altitude sickness that affects the lungs and brain. Such edemas are often fatal unless treated rapidly with oxygen and descent. They are also know as high-altitude pulmonary edema (HAPE) and high-altitude cerebral edema (HACE).

fixed rope A static (nonstretching) climbing rope that is attached to ice screws and snow stakes and left in place on the mountain at difficult or steep sections.

glacier A very slow-moving river of ice.

hypothermia A serious lowering of the body's core temperature.

Gamow bag An airtight nylon cylinder in which the pressure can be raised with a foot pump to the equivalent of descending several hundred feet. Used for treating altitude sickness.

Gompa Tibetan Buddhist monastery.

Gore-Tex The predominant brand of waterproof yet breathable fabric that is used in mountaineering applications such as tents, shell clothing, and sleeping bag covers.

hydration system A collapsible water bottle (that can be carried in your pack) with a long, flexible hose that enables you to drink easily when trekking or climbing.

Jumar see ascender.

kata A white silk or muslin Buddhist ceremonial scarf given as a gift to someone setting out on a journey or climb.

Khumbu The Khumbu is the region of Eastern Nepal that includes the headwaters of the Dud Kosi (Milk River), which are above 9,000 feet (2,744 meters). The Khumbu is the home of the famous Sherpa people and contains three of the world's seven highest mountains: Everest, Lhotse, and Cho Oyu.

Lama A Buddhist monk; the master.

mantra A string of papers containing invocations and prayers enclosed in prayer wheels.

monsoon The rainy period from June to late September when there is rainfall virtually every day.

namaste The most common greeting in Nepal, said with the palms of your hands pressed together in front of your chest. The translation is "I bow to the god in you."

Nepal Nepal is a tiny landlocked country sandwiched between India and China. Much of Nepal sits astride the Himalayas, the largest chain of mountains in the world.

porter Anyone whose job is carrying a load for money. Porters come from many different ethnic groups. Many farmers work as porters when they are not needed in their fields.

prayer flags Said to bring happiness, long life, and prosperity to anyone in their vicinity. Each lungta (flag) is imprinted with mantras (prayers) and good luck symbols such as the winged horse. The five colors (yellow, green, red, white, and blue) are always hung in the same order, representing the elements of earth, water, fire, cloud, and sky.

puja A religious ritual or observance.

self-arrest A technique for stopping a sliding fall down a steep ice slope using the pick of an ice axe.

sirdar The head Sherpa, or organizer.

stupa A hemispherical Buddhist shrine.

Sources

Organizations

The American Mountain Guides Association
Phone (303) 271-1206
http://www.amga.com/info/choose
_mtn_guide.htm

Himalayan Explorers Club
P.O. Box 3665
Boulder, CO 80307
Phone (303) 998-0101
Fax (303) 998-1007
http://www.hec.org

National Outdoor Leadership School
(NOLS)
288 Main St.
Lander, WY 82520
Phone (307) 332-5300
http://www.nols.edu/NOLSHome.html

Outward Bound
100 Mystery Point Road
Garrison, NY 10524
Phone (888) 882-6863 or (845) 424-4000
Fax (845) 424-8286
http://www.outwardbound.org/

Clubs

The American Alpine Club
710 Tenth St., Ste. 100
Golden, CO 80401
Phone (303) 384-0110
Fax (303) 384-0111
http://www.AmericanAlpineClub.org/

The Appalachia Mountain Club
5 Joy St.
Boston, MA 02108
Phone (617) 523-0636
Fax (617) 523-0722
http://www.outdoors.org/

The Colorado Mountain Club
American Mountaineering Center
710 10th St.
Golden, CO80401
Phone (303) 279-3080
Fax (303) 279-9690
http://www.coloradomountainclub.org/

The Mazamas
909 NW 19th Ave.
Portland, OR 97209
Phone (503) 227-2345
http://www.mazamas.org

The Mountaineers
300 3rd Ave.

West Seattle, WA 98119
Phone (206) 284-6310 or (800) 573-8484
Fax (206) 284-4977
http://www.mountaineers.org/

Climbing Gyms

For addresses of U.S. rock-climbing gyms:
http://www.climbing.com/Pages/rockgyms
00.html

Guide Companies

Alpine Ascents International
121 Mercer St.
Seattle, WA 98109
Phone (206) 378-1927
Fax (206) 378-1937
http://www.AlpineAscents.com

American Alpine Institute
1515 12th St., Ste. N-4
Bellingham, WA 98225
Phone (360) 671-1505
http://www.mtnguide.com/

International Mountain Guides
P.O. Box 246
Ashford, WA 98304
Phone (360) 569-2604
Fax (360) 569-0824
http://www.mountainguides.com/

Books

Bernbaum, Edwin. *Sacred Mountains of the World*. The Sierra Club, 1990.

Coburn, Broughton. *Triumph on Everest: A Photobiography of Sir Edmund Hillary*. National Geographic Society, 2000.

Broughton Coburn, Tim Cahill, and David Breashears. *Everest: Mountain Without Mercy*. National Geographic Society, 1997.

Diemberger, Kurt. *The Endless Knot: K2 Mountain of Dreams and Destiny*. The Mountaineers, 1991.

Gilman, Peter, ed. *Everest: The Best Writing and Pictures from Seventy Years of Human Endeavor*. Little, Brown, 1993.

Graydon, Don and Kurt Hanson. *Mountaineering: The Freedom of the Hills*. The Mountaineers, 1997.

Hillary, Edmund. *High Adventure*. Hodder & Stoughton, 1955.

Jenkins, Steve. *The Top of the World: Climbing Mount Everest*. Houghton Mifflin, 1999.

McGuinness, Jamie. *Trekking in the Everest Region*. Trailblazer, 1998.

Platt, Richard. *Everest: Reaching the World's Highest Peak*. Dorling Kindersley,

1990.

Salkeld, Audrey ed. *World Mountaineering*. Little, Brown, 1999.

Salkeld, Audrey and Conrad Anker. *Mystery on Everest: A Photobiography of George Mallory*. National Geographic Society, 2000.

Maps

Mount Everest. 1:50,000 Boston Museum of Science/Swiss Foundation of Alpine Research, National Geographic Society.

Everest Base Camp Trekking Map. 1:250,000, National Geographic Society

Available from AdventurousTraveler.com
Phone (800) 282-3963 Fax (800) 677-1821
245 S. Champlain Street
Burlington, VT 05401
http://www.adventuroustraveler.com/

Magazines

Climbing Magazine
326 Highway 133, Ste. 190
Carbondale, CO 81623
Phone (800) 493-4569
http://www.climbing.com/

Outside Magazine
400 Market St.
Santa Fe, NM 87501
http://www.outsidemagazine.com/

Rock & Ice
5455 Spine Rd., Mezzanine A
Boulder, CO 80301
Phone (303) 499-8410
Fax (303) 530-3729
http://www.rockandice.com/

Web sites

Jonathan Chester / Extreme Images
http://www.extremeimages.com/

Everest News.com
http://www.everestnews.com

Himalayas—Where Earth Meets the Sky
http://library.thinkquest.org/10131/

Mount Everest.Net
http://www.mnteverest.net/

The Mountain Zone
http://mountainzone.com

Museum of Science Boston
http://www.mos.org/Everest/

Nova
http://www.pbs.org/wgbh/nova/everest/

Steponline—Nancy Feagin
http://www.steponline.com/everest/

To Katharine and Cormac — May your lives be full of adventure

Acknowledgments

Special thanks to Kirsty Melville, my partner in life and work, who first dreamed up the book and shared the load along the way; Catherine Jacobes, for her inspired design and creative input at all stages of the project; and the team at Tricycle Press, Nicole Geiger, Summer Laurie, and Laura Mancuso, who helped ensure that the book reached the summit.

No book like this can be produced in a vacuum. I would also like to thank my copyeditor, Beverly McGuire and Dan, Sam, and Alex Morrison and Spencer, and Adam Sherman for their very helpful reader's comments,

I am very grateful to the members of the National Federation of the Blind (NFB) 2001 Everest Expedition, particularly Eric Alexander, Luis Benitez, Bradford Bull, Reba Bull, Sherman Bull, Kevin Chirilla, Jeff Evans, Steve Gipe, Didrik Johnck, Kim Johnson, Charley Mace, Chris Morris, Michael O'Donnell, Maurice Peret, Matthew Sanner, Pasquale (PV) Scaturro, Kami Tenzing Sherpa, and Erik Weihenmayer. Thanks also to Glenn Timmons and Bill Waite of Newport Productions, who made it possible for me to visit Nepal again. Lastly, thanks to all my many climbing partners over the years, who have helped me reach my own summits and get back home safely.

Front Cover: Bradford Bull (right) and his father, Sherman Bull (who became the oldest person to reach the summit of Everest on May 25, 2001). Photograph © 2001 Bradford Bull Collection.

Back Cover: Everest Base Camp at night, Photograph © 2001 Jonathan Chester / Extreme Images.

End Papers: Prayer flags at Everest Base Camp (front) Mani stones at Namche Bazaar (back)

Text copyright © 2002 by Jonathan Chester

1 2 3 4 5 6 — 06 05 04 03 02

Photographs
All photos by Jonathan Chester / Extreme Images, except
Bradford Bull, front cover, victory
Didrik Johnck, crevasse
Chris Curry/ Hedgehog House, route
Nick Groves / Hedgehog House, Quomolanga

Map
Nepal Elevation Map © 1999 Maps.com

Greystone Books
A division of Douglas & McIntyre Ltd.
2323 Quebec Street, Suite 201
Vancouver, British Columbia V5T 4S7
www.greystonebooks.com

Design by Catherine Jacobes
Typset in Base Nine and Domestos

National Library of Canada Cataloguing in Publication Data
Chester, Jonathan.
  The young adventurer's guide to Everest.

ISBN 1-55054-934-0

 1. Everest, Mount (China and Nepal)—Guidebooks. I. Title.
DS495.8.E9C53 2002   915.49604   C2001-911549-0

The publisher gratefully acknowledges the support of the Canada Council and of the British Columbia Ministry of Tourism, Small Business and Culture. The publisher also wishes to acknowledge the financial support of the Government of Canada through the Book Publishing Industry Development Program (BPIDP) for its publishing activities.

First printing 2002
Printed in Hong Kong